I'm Allergic to Nuts

Susan McCune

I0808449

Rosen REAL READERS

Rosen Classroom™
New York

My name is James. I went to school yesterday. I brought my lunch to school.

I packed a **peanut** butter and jelly sandwich. At lunch I ate my sandwich.

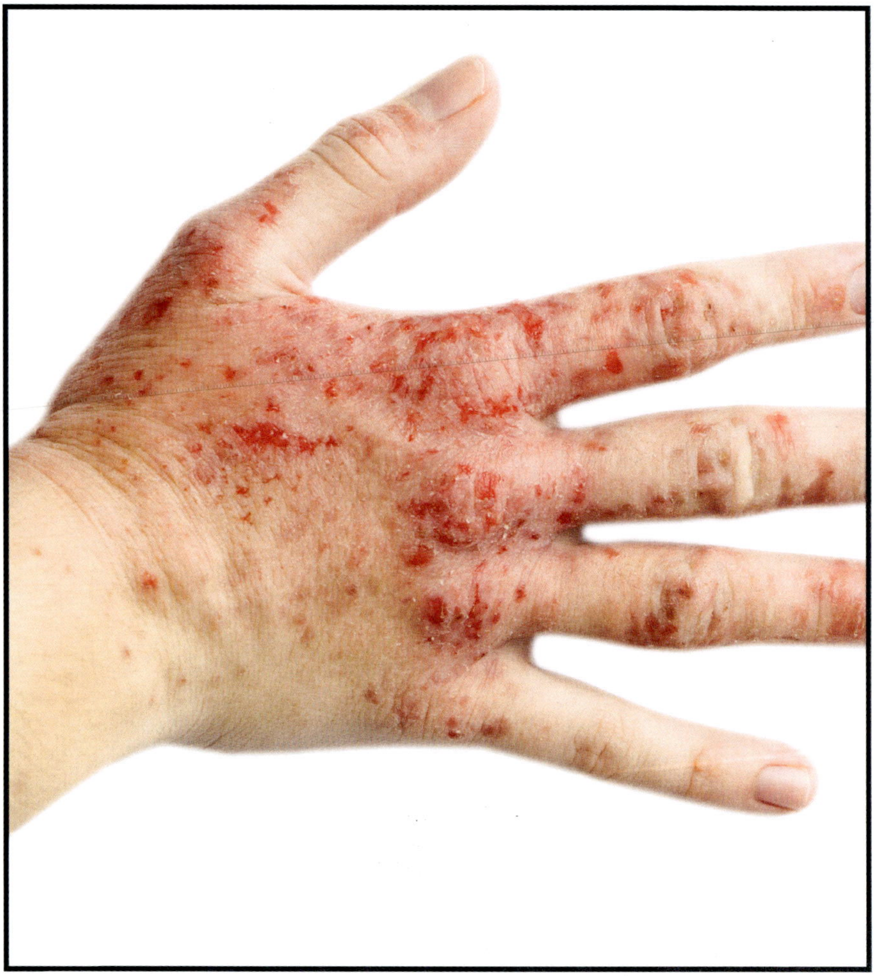

A few minutes later, I felt sick. My body felt itchy too. I saw a **rash** on my hand.

My mom took me to the doctor. The doctor said that I am **allergic** to nuts.

She said that many people are allergic to nuts. The doctor said that I must not have nuts in my **diet.** If I eat nuts, I will get sick.

Nuts are in many different foods. I cannot eat nuts. I cannot eat peanut butter. I cannot eat foods cooked in peanut oil.

When my mom goes shopping, she looks for foods without nuts. She reads the labels on the boxes.

Some food labels say, "Contains no nuts." These are the foods that I can eat.

When I go to eat in a restaurant, I look for food on the menu that is nut-free. There are a lot of choices.

In the school cafeteria, I order food without nuts. The lunch lady always has meals without nuts!

Glossary

allergic Having an allergy to something.

diet The food that a person eats.

peanut A nut with a thin shell that grows under the ground and that can be eaten.

rash A group of red spots on the skin that is caused by a reaction to something.